Gh Encounters

Chilling True Stories of Ghost Manifestations and Haunted Houses

Conrad Bauer

Disclaimer and Terms of Use

Effort has been made to ensure that the information in this book is accurate and complete. However, the author and the publisher do not warrant the accuracy of the information, text, and graphics contained within the book due to the rapidly changing nature of science, research, known and unknown facts, and internet. The author and the publisher do not hold any responsibility for errors, omissions, or contrary interpretation of the subject matter herein. This book is presented solely for motivational and informational purposes only.

ISBN: 978-1725126459

Printed in the United States

Contents

Apparitions from Beyond

Ghosts, phantoms, apparitions from beyond—not everyone sees them, but those who do don't soon forget it. But what *are* these strange visions of the night? And what do they mean? Accounts of ghostly encounters are as old as human history itself. In fact, one of the oldest documented reports of a ghost comes from the Bible.

This ghost story took place when the first ruler of Israel, King Saul, visited the Witch of Endor and asked that ancient medium to summon the spirit of the prophet Samuel. The summoning was successful, but Samuel's shade was none too happy about being disturbed and told the king in no uncertain terms not to try it again. The moral of the story seems to be that ghosts *do* exist, but they are far too dangerous for mortal man to trifle with and are better avoided than pursued.

Despite this biblical prohibition, contact with those on the other side has continued unabated throughout the centuries. And during this long chronology of ghostly happenings, many theories have been postulated to answer the eternal question of who or what these apparitions from the beyond actually are.

The first and simplest is that ghost stories are nothing more than the product of an overactive imagination. According to this theory, no matter how incredible an encounter with a supposed spirit may seem, the entire experience takes place in our own minds. Ghosts don't come from beyond so much as from our own subconscious.

Of course, writing the phenomenon off as a mere mental fancy is much easier for someone who hasn't experienced it than it is for those who have actually lived through it. And besides, this theory does a poor job of explaining the many instances of multiple witnesses to supposed spectral events. If you don't believe in the supernatural, the only real explanation for such cases would be mass hallucination—and the jury is still out on whether such a thing even exists!

But the best argument against the simple explanation remains the testimony of those who say they've lived to tell the tale. And so, this book is filled to the brim with just such tales of encounters with ghostly apparitions from beyond. Read on and decide for yourself just how credible you find these incredible stories of the spirits!

A Case of Ghostly Roommates

Manuel Varo had just moved into a rental home that had recently been renovated due to a fire and turned into sectioned-off apartments. He shared the space with a housemate named Dave. Manuel's apartment was cozy and had all of the amenities he'd been promised—but strange ghostly happenings in the late-night hours made the high-speed internet come off as a sorry consolation. The strangeness began shortly after Manuel put his things away.

First he began to notice the sound of cabinet doors in his kitchen rattling loudly when no one was in the room. It sounded as if someone was quickly opening and closing the cabinets at random. Yet whenever Manuel went into the kitchen to investigate, he would find all the cabinet doors shut and the room totally quiet, as if he had imagined the whole thing.

In the following days, whatever was haunting his apartment grew tired of these subtle little games of hide-and-seek and began presenting itself to him more forthrightly. At 3:30 one

3

morning, Manuel was jarred awake by the sound of his radio blasting at full volume in the house's common area. This was an old-school analog stereo, and there was no way for it to turn on unless someone physically turned the radio dial. Upset and suspicious, Manuel went and pounded on Dave's door. His equally irked housemate, however, was adamant that he hadn't gone anywhere near Manuel's radio and demanded that Manuel "chill out" so that he could get some sleep.

Manuel went back to bed, but for the rest of the week he noticed periodic disturbances wherever he was in the apartment. He would often see lights flickering on and off for no apartment reason when he walked by, and he would often hear loud thuds from the wall next to where he sat. The inexplicable thudding really rattled him, and Manuel soon concluded that whatever was behind it all was intelligently motivated. The banging was too well timed to be anything other than a planned intrusion, deliberately designed to create the greatest possible effect.

This became particularly clear when Manuel was home alone one night watching a movie—only to be beset by the sudden thumping of his ghostly intruder. He was watching an action film in which one character had pulled a gun on the other. Completely absorbed in the drama of the movie, right when the character was about to pull the trigger, Manuel heard a loud boom on the wall behind his sofa. He nearly jumped out of his skin and his heart started pounding as if he himself had been shot! He didn't know whether his ghostly tormentor was somewhere laughing about the whole thing, but he did know that this was an obvious attempt to scare him.

But even though the ghost clearly wanted to play pranks on Manuel, for the time being, it wanted to keep its identity a secret. Manuel realized this when he tried to look up the history of the house on his laptop (no doubt looking forward to that free high-speed internet with which his landlord had enticed him to sign the lease). Whenever he tried to find information about the previous tenants, his computer would either freeze, crash, or experience an abrupt power failure.

Manuel had just purchased the laptop, so his first thought was that he'd gotten a defective unit. He immediately took it back to the store and had them look at it. The store employees ran the computer through a series of diagnostic tests to see what was wrong, but after several hours of looking they couldn't find any problems and gave the device a clean bill of health. Manuel insisted that there must be something wrong with his laptop for it to keep shorting out like it had. The store clerks, though, were just as adamant that there was nothing wrong, and a shouting match ensued. Getting fed up with the whole situation, the manager came over and actually ordered the frustrated Manuel to "leave and not come back" because there was "absolutely nothing wrong" with his computer.

After returning home and calming down, Manuel began to consider whether the absence of a technical explanation for his laptop trouble meant that there might be some kind of presence in his home. And upon accepting this realization, he began to speculate that whatever this presence was, it just might have something to do with the fire that had occurred there.

Manuel was now intrigued enough to do his own detective work, and following the lead of ghost sleuths he had seen on television, he began to seek out EVPs from the spirits haunting his home. EVP stands for "electronic voice phenomenon", the alleged ability of audio recording equipment to capture disembodied voices. The voices are not heard as the recording is being made; they are only discovered upon playback. The technique remains controversial, with some castigating it as nothing more than the haphazard capturing of random

5

background noise. Others, however, have claimed some rather startling results—and soon Manuel would be one of them.

When he listened to the first recordings, Manuel could only hear feedback and possibly some incoherent "growling". But when his housemate entered the picture, things started to get serious. Dave, thinking the whole thing was a funny gag, yelled out to any spirits in the room, "Go to the light, damn it—just go to the freaking light!" When the two replayed this part of the tape, they were astonished to hear a deep male voice shout in response, "No! Stay away from the light! Don't go to the light!"

As the investigation progressed, Manuel, who at first had been cautious of provoking the ghost, was cajoled by his housemate to join in on the taunts. Tired of Dave calling him a scaredy-cat, Manuel downed a couple of beer bottles of liquid courage and began to openly insult the apparitions he believed to be haunting his home. At one point he even opened up the box of pizza that he and his housemate were sharing and asked, "Hey ghosts! Would you like a slice of pizza? Oh, wait, you can't— because you're dead!"

This careless remark would literally come back to haunt Manuel and Dave later that night when they reviewed the recording. Their (significantly soberer) blood ran cold when they came to the part where Manuel taunted the spirits that they couldn't have any pizza because they were dead. A little girl's voice responded with marked annoyance, "So what? Who cares?"

Manuel was terrified to hear this ghostly rebuke from the other side. The fun and games were over now, and he realized he had something serious on his hands that wouldn't go away on its own. He was only too right. The ghostly mischief was about to get violent.

6

A few days later, Manuel, trying to get his mind off of the haunting, invited his girlfriend over for dinner and a movie. Things went fine at first, until in the middle of the movie, one of Manuel's paintings came crashing down off the wall with no apparent cause. There was nothing to shake the wall, there was no air blowing through any window, and yet this painting was violently torn down, slamming onto the floor with such force that the frame shattered into several pieces. Manuel certainly didn't appreciate this treatment of his artwork, but not wishing to frighten his girlfriend (or himself!), he tried his best to laugh it off, joking about his home having some kind of "friendly neighborhood poltergeist".

His girlfriend apparently wasn't convinced, though, and quickly found an excuse to cut the evening short. Demoralized, depressed, and defeated, Manuel walked his departing lover to her car, said goodbye, and turned to go back to his haunted home. Staring up into the windows of his foreboding abode, he was momentarily tempted to get in his car and just drive off— just go somewhere else far away from whatever was causing all this turmoil in his life.

But not yet able to summon the nerve to make a break for it, Manuel took a deep breath, walked up the rickety steps to his porch, and went back inside. No sooner had he shut the door behind him than a horseshoe that had been nailed to the wall tore free from its moorings and was hurled right at his head. He ducked and narrowly avoided getting brained, but the horseshoe still gave him a considerable gash on his scalp as it glanced off the top of his head. He knew now that these ghosts were serious, and that they wouldn't rest until they inflicted some sort of major bodily harm upon him.

Meanwhile, Dave had begun hearing banging, footsteps, and dragging sounds in his room at night. It scared the crap out of him as well, and due to these terrifying attacks by their ghostly "third housemate" the two grown men decided to camp out together in sleeping bags in the living room! Afraid to sleep alone, Manuel and Dave decided to literally watch each other's backs by sleeping back to back on the living room floor!

During one of these late-night vigils, the two were startled to hear the mouse of Manuel's computer clicking and moving on its own. To their amazement it seemed as if an unseen hand was working the controls. Then, as they stared in astonishment, a newspaper article popped onto the screen. The mouse ceased its uncanny movement, and Manuel gathered his courage and stepped closer to the screen to read the words illuminated on its surface. The newspaper report revealed the details of a fire that had occurred at the house ten years prior. Caught completely unaware, the residents were killed in the blaze. One man was found burned to death in the hallway valiantly trying to reach his two young daughters, and sadly, those two girls perished hiding under their bed.

As he read the words, Manuel immediately wondered if the deep voice they had heard on the EVP warning "Don't go to the light!" was the father. The other voice that responded to his taunts with "Who cares!" was perhaps one of the little girls. Did these ghosts know that they were dead? Did they not care? Were they still listening to their dad's instructions as he forbid them to "go to the light"—deciding instead to haunt the Earth as a ghostly family?

As these thoughts raced through Manuel's mind, the computer which had conveyed the spirits' revelation eerily shorted out once again. It refused to turn on again until several hours later. Under normal circumstances, Manuel would have assumed the problem to be a dead battery, or at worst a virus. Ghostly tampering from the other side certainly would not have been the first thing to come to mind! But this was the strange reality in which he now lived.

The fact that the previously secretive ghosts had now revealed their biggest secret made Manuel feel even more uneasy. He felt like the spirits were becoming intimately acquainted with him, and the very thought made him feel sick to his stomach. And as the 3:00 AM blasts of radio, the pounding, and the falling objects continued, he was not only sick of it, he was also becoming very angry himself. Manuel wasn't sure if he was just mad at what was happening, or if all the negative energy of the visiting earthbound spirits was rubbing off on him, but he perpetually felt as if he himself was about to explode in rage.

One day he reached his limit and began yelling at the unseen phantoms, "Listen up! You guys are dead! You died! Go away! You don't belong here!" Manuel then came up with a special threat for his visitors, in case they didn't heed his words: "And if you don't leave, I'm going to get a priest in here to send you packing to wherever it is you need to go!"

As soon as he said it, Manuel regretted it. The very walls of his home seemed to shake with anger, and a cold chill filled the room. His eyes were drawn to a light on the ceiling which began to grow brighter and brighter. It was as if a power surge was occurring to just that one light bulb, making it seem as if it were about to overload and burst. But just as the light seemed ready to blow, it abruptly dimmed.

Such frightful activity continued to increase in intensity—until one morning it reached its terrible climax. Manuel and his housemate woke up to smoke filling the house. Jumping out of his bed, Manuel immediately saw the source of the smoke. Curtains had been torn from the window and flung down on top of a kerosene heater. The edges of the curtains were frayed, melted, and smoking—and if they had been left in place much longer, the whole home no doubt would have caught fire.

It seemed to Manuel that his threat to evict his ghostly housemates had failed. Instead of being afraid that he would force them to leave, they seemed intent on forcing *him* to join them on the other side! He didn't like the idea that he was being bullied out of his own home by a bunch of ghosts, but he didn't want to become a ghost, either! Knowing that he couldn't stay any longer, Manuel packed his things, broke his lease, and never looked back.

The Home of Her Dreams

For most of us, the swimming pool is a place to relax and forget about the struggles of everyday life. But for a young mother-to-be named Julie, this place of relaxation would become a focal point for horror.

She and her husband, Craig, had recently moved into a new home—new to them, anyway, but actually very old, dating back at least 150 years. Nevertheless, Julie had fallen in love with the house upon first laying eyes on it, and the asking price seemed very reasonable considering all the recent renovations. Even though the home had some age on it, it had been given a facelift and several upgrades. It even had a luxurious backyard swimming pool that had been put in during more recent decades. Julie thought that she was getting a real bargain as she and her husband signed the final pieces of paperwork for the purchase—but in reality, she was getting more than she had bargained *for*.

Nevertheless, Julie was excited as the couple moved into their new home and began to explore every single nook and cranny as they unpacked. During this exploratory process Julie discovered a little baby shoe shoved back on the top shelf of the closet. Curious, she fetched a step ladder and retrieved the shoe. It was a bit of an odd find, but Julie, who was pregnant and expecting her own little one, took it as a sign of good things to come.

At first Julie and Craig were very happy in their new home and considered themselves lucky to have gotten such a good deal on such a spacious and well cared for piece of property. But the strangeness that surrounded the abode began to manifest after just a few days. Julie was swimming in the pool one night, as she had done almost every night since they moved in, when she thought she saw an object submerged in the deep end. Diving down to retrieve it, she nearly gasped underwater at what she saw. It was a baby shoe, just like the one she had found in the closet.

Taking the shoe in hand, she immediately marched back into the house and went to the bookshelf where she had placed the original shoe. The shoe was gone. Realizing that the shoe that she found in the pool was the same one that was supposed to be on the bookcase, a shiver ran down her spine as she wondered how it could have moved from one place to another. The only rational explanation was that Craig had tossed it into the pool as some kind of prank—but that would have been extremely out of character for her straight-laced, no-nonsense husband.

Nevertheless, it was the only lead she had to go on. So the now very much disturbed Julie stormed into the study where Craig was working in order to get some answers. Holding the dripping wet shoe in front of his face, she demanded, "Craig! Did you drop this shoe into the pool while I was swimming?" Craig, however, was taken completely aback by the accusation and professed complete ignorance. Seeing the sincerity on his face, Julie had no choice but to believe him.

With the only rational explanation for the incident denied her, Julie was forced to conclude that something very strange was happening. Even though she didn't always go to mass, Julie was a devout Catholic, and it was to her faith she turned when she was looking for answers. She called up a local priest and arranged for him to come and bless their residence.

The priest began walking from room to room praying and asking God to sanctify the home. Nearly as soon as he started, Julie felt a shift in the atmosphere. Everything seemed to change, and an oppressive presence could be felt all throughout the house. As the negative feelings increased, the priest abruptly stopped praying and excused himself to go to the bathroom. From the other side of the door, Julie could hear him vomiting. Something had clearly shaken up this man of the cloth— something that he could not control. After a few minutes, the bathroom door opened and the priest, with bloodshot eyes and a stone-cold expression, walked right past her and headed straight out the front door. Julie followed him to his car, but he left without saying a word.

Stunned, Julie waited until later that evening to telephone the church to find out what had happened. But when she was connected to the priest's office, she heard only silence and then the sound of someone hanging up the phone. What was happening in her home? Was it so bad that even the Church didn't want to get involved? Julie didn't know, but she decided not to tell her husband about it. Craig not only didn't believe in ghosts, he was also an avowed atheist, and she knew he wouldn't appreciate her having a priest over to bless the house.

Julie wasn't sure if the priest's truncated blessing had helped expel any of the negativity from the house. But things were quiet for the next few weeks, and she began to tell herself that everything was back to normal. But this peace of mind would not last.

When Craig left on a business trip, Julie was left alone for the weekend. She didn't like it, but she accepted that it was a part of her husband's job and was determined to grin and bear it as best she could. That Saturday morning Julie was in the kitchen cooking some scrambled eggs when she heard the pitter-patter of little footsteps behind her. Cringing at the thought of an intruder, she gasped and turned around, dropping her spatula onto the floor in the process. But there was no sign of anyone in the house. Catching her breath, she told herself that it must have been her imagination and bent down to pick up the spatula.

And then she gasped again, because all over the kitchen floor she now noticed tiny puddles, as if a small child with wet feet had walked through the room. Astonished, she left the spatula where it lay and got up and followed the trail of puddles. They led her from the kitchen all the way to the upstairs bedroom. As soon as she reached the top of the stairs, she could have sworn she saw someone quickly run past her out of the corner of her eye. Yet when she turned around, there was no one to be seen.

The strangeness intensified later that night when Julie woke to the sensation of a hand gently caressing her hair. Her first thought was that her husband had arrived home early from his trip. As she shook the sleep from her eyes and rolled over in bed, she started to welcome him.

"Hey, Craig—"

She stopped herself in mid-sentence when she saw that there was no one there. She frantically flipped on the lamp on the nightstand and confirmed that Craig wasn't home. She was still all alone in the house. So, who was it that she had so clearly felt touching her hair? Needless to say, Julie had an incredibly hard time getting back to sleep that night—and by the time her husband actually did come back from his trip, she was close to a complete nervous breakdown.

When Craig returned, she began to plead with him that they needed to leave the house as soon as possible. Her husband wasn't having it, though. He chastised his panicked wife for being hysterical and told her she was just having nightmares. But even though he didn't believe her, Craig felt sorry for Julie. He promised not to go on any more business trips out of town, saying that he would stay nearby so she would be able to call upon him whenever she needed to.

A few days later the doorbell rang and the couple answered it to find none other than the priest, accompanied by another man. Craig, of course, had no idea of what had previously transpired with the aborted blessing. He immediately asked who the men were and what they wanted. The priest refused to answer any questions, however. Bizarrely, he simply repeated the same phrase in Latin over and over, "Puer in ila cupit! Puer in ila cupit!"

Equal parts annoyed and disturbed, Craig demanded to know, "What is he saying? I don't know what you're saying!"

Julie brushed past her husband and asked the other man, "What is it? What is he trying to tell us?"

The man responded somberly, "Well… it's Latin. Ever since he left this house, all he speaks is Latin." Shaking his head, he added, "He's saying, 'She wants the baby. She wants the baby.'"

Immensely frustrated and perturbed, Craig pointed at his wife's now visibly pregnant belly and angrily snapped, "Yeah, right! Of course she wants the baby! Now get the hell out of here and leave us alone!"

As Craig slammed the door in the Catholic clergymen's faces, Julie chastised him, "Craig! You didn't have to do that!"

Craig angrily retorted, "Look—I don't know who these people are or what you've been doing while I've been away, but it has to stop!" He then stormed back up to his study, where he remained for the rest of the evening.

Despite this flair up of marital tensions, things seemed to go back to normal after this incident. No further strange events occurred, and the couple began to really enjoy their house and the time they spent together in it. Craig, when he wasn't working on projects from his job, found the time to spruce up the room they had chosen for the baby's nursery. His pride and joy at the moment was the baby monitor he had installed, which allowed him to listen to and watch the room remotely on his laptop and phone.

But he soon got quite a surprise when he opened the window for the monitor and saw something he wasn't prepared to see. Standing in the corner of the dark room was a figure with its back turned. Craig couldn't make out the figure clearly because it was so dark, but it was obvious that *someone* was there. Thinking it must be his wife and wondering why she was standing in the corner like that, he shouted up at her, "Hey Julie! What are you doing up there in the dark?"

Julie immediately came out of the kitchen and responded, "Doing what up where?"

Craig, seeing his wife standing right in front of him, quickly looked back at the monitor, but the shadowy figure was gone. Feeling a slight tinge of fear as he realized that there was no way his wife could have been in that nursery, Craig could only rationalize it by questioning his own sanity—an option which he decided to embrace wholeheartedly. He convinced himself that overwork and lack of sleep were causing him to hallucinate. And knowing that his wife was already on edge, he was determined not to speak one word about the incident to her.

But even though Craig was willing to ignore the apparitions, Julie was not. And in any event there was no way that the next incident to occur could be cast aside as the work of her imagination. Craig was working late, and Julie had decided to spend the rest of the evening swimming in the pool. Out of the corner of her eye she saw someone else swimming right there with her. It was the figure of a woman with long dark hair. Julie turned in terror toward the figure, but it simply vanished— disappeared as if it were never there in the first place.

Desperately needing answers, Julie jumped out of the pool and ran straight to her husband's laptop, which had been left open on the kitchen table. She began googling information on the home's history and its previous residents and quickly found out the real horror story behind her home.

About 10 years before, a young family had lived in the house, a husband and wife and their two-year-old daughter. The family had apparently hit some hard times, however, and the husband left after filing for divorce. The young woman was so distraught that she made a horrible decision. She decided that if her husband didn't want to be married to her, then she would take both herself and her daughter away from him permanently. She did this by drowning her daughter and then herself in the home's outdoor swimming pool.

Julie immediately telephoned Craig to tell him what she had found out. Once he was on the other end, she demanded that they leave the house—and leave it at once. Craig knew that his wife was serious, but he wasn't quite prepared to drop everything and run. He told her to "sit tight" and promised to discuss the whole thing further when he got home. Since he was working the late shift, though, he wouldn't be home until about two in the morning, which left Julie alone with the spirits that inhabited her household for several more hours.

Julie went to bed that night full of fear and anxiety, but she did eventually fall asleep. She woke up just an hour or so later, however, to receive the fright of her life. She opened her eyes to see a deathly pale woman with dark black hair lying in bed next to her. The woman was covered in water and suddenly began gagging as if she were drowning, spitting up pool water all over the bed. Julie screamed as loud as she had ever screamed in her life, and somewhere in the middle of those screams, the water-logged phantom disappeared.

Julie had finally had enough, and she frantically began to pack up all of their belongings. And as soon as her husband got home she convinced him that they needed to leave that very night. And so, with both of them running on pure adrenalin and no sleep, they lugged what belongings they could into their SUV and checked into a local motel, never looking back at their former dream home turned nightmare.

The Monster in the Closet

Times were tough for little Bobby Monroe. His mom and dad had just decided to call it quits on their seven-year marriage, and the five-year-old was being forced to move away from his old neighborhood and friends and into a new home several miles away.

His mother, Marcy, who was a teacher, had just gotten a job as an instructional assistant at a school on the other side of town, and the position came with the rare amenity of employee housing. Another added perk of the move for Marcy was the fact that her sister Brenda lived nearby. As a new single parent, Marcy really needed some family support for her and her son, and Brenda became a big part of their lives from the beginning, helping them move in and unpack their things.

It was Brenda who first witnessed the house's strange effect on Bobby. The two had been busy going room to room, exploring the place, when Bobby suddenly walked toward a door in the hallway. It led to a small closet that Brenda and Marcy had completely overlooked, but Bobby walked right up to it and opened it up. Inside he found a strange beat-up old doll. It was one of the old "crying baby" dolls from a couple of decades ago, the ones that cried when you shook them. The cry that these dolls produced was never exactly endearing, but the sound that this particular doll made was downright creepy.

Nevertheless, Bobby was immediately enamored with the doll. From then on he took it with him everywhere he went. The other odd habit that Bobby picked up was playing in the large walk-in closet in his bedroom. His mother would find him just sitting in the closet with the door shut, playing with the eerie doll he had found.

One day Marcy discovered the usually quiet Bobby in what seemed to be a long and animated conversation with someone as he sat in the closet. She opened the closet door, and Bobby immediately ceased speaking as his mother inquired, "What are you doing in there? Are you talking to a friend?" At first Marcy wasn't overly concerned with the idea of her son having an imaginary friend. She was quite used to seeing that kind of behavior in the kids she taught at school, so she didn't really think too much of it.

But as the days progressed, she noticed an increased difference in her son's demeanor. One night, as she was putting away the dinner dishes, she noticed her son furiously drawing pictures at the kitchen table—and what he was illustrating was not exactly the stuff of dinnertime conversation. He was drawing rapidly, and in one sitting he had managed to create several deeply disturbing depictions. They showed a little boy chained up, people with their hands cut off, and a man crying tears of blood.

Marcy had never seen anything like this come from her son before. Just where did this otherwise normal five-year-old get the idea to draw such things? Marcy discussed the issue with Brenda, who was deeply concerned with the state of mind of both her nephew and her sister. Thinking that some fresh air and time to herself could do Marcy some good, she volunteered to babysit Bobby the following Saturday.

Brenda looked forward to this opportunity to hang out and bond with her nephew, but she ended up being rather disappointed by Bobby's lack of enthusiasm. As soon as she arrived, Bobby immediately picked up the spooky doll and took it to the closet, refusing to come out. Brenda was a little dismayed by the behavior, but she tried to take it in stride. As the day wore on, however, and Bobby continued to stay in the closet and the doll continued to make annoying sounds, she reached a breaking point.

She stormed up to Bobby's bedroom, opened the closet door and took the doll away from Bobby. She then opened up the part of the doll where the batteries should have been—but found it to be empty. There were no batteries in this "talking doll". Throwing the doll down on the floor, Brenda ran back downstairs and remained there until Marcy got back. When her sister came home, she told her all about what had happened. To Brenda's disbelief, Marcy tried to play down the whole thing. She insisted that there must be a rational explanation and suggested that perhaps the batteries were just hidden somewhere else inside the doll.

Sticking to this skeptical script, Marcy continued to go about her business in the home, pushing aside any suspicions she may have had. Then one day she was sweeping the floor in the kitchen when she got the strange feeling that something wasn't right with her son. You can call it mother's intuition or just a general forewarning, but something was rattling the alarm bells in Marcy's mind. She immediately when to Bobby's closet and found him sitting silently inside with his hands covered in blood. She didn't know where the blood had come from, if he had injured himself, or if something else had happened—but she knew that she had to get him out of that closet.

After taking him to the bathroom to wash up, she checked him head to toe for scrapes, cuts, or sores, but found none. After this, she sternly instructed her son to not play in the closet anymore. She then conferred with her sister about the whole ordeal, and the two both agreed to nail the closet shut so Bobby wouldn't be getting into it anymore. They spent the following evening driving long, sturdy nails into the closet door. Once Brenda went home, Marcy put Bobby to bed and then went to her own room and drifted off to sleep.

Her sleep was fitful at best, and she woke up with a start before the early morning hours were out. All throughout the night she had been having disturbing nightmares of seeing her son covered in blood, or alternatively chained to the walls. She confided with her sister again the next morning, and Brenda agreed to stay with them for a few days just to make sure that everything was alright.

During her stay, Brenda became increasingly convinced that the talking doll Bobby carried around with him must have something to do with the strange happenings in the home. She wasn't sure why, but she had a gut feeling that the doll was somehow "evil" and had to be removed. One night when Bobby was properly distracted, she managed to sneak into his room and take the doll. She then took it outside, poured gasoline on it, and lit a match. The doll was melted and destroyed. Brenda felt horrible for burning her nephew's doll, but she also felt certain that the heavy, oppressive atmosphere in the home would lift after she did so.

At first it seemed that her theory had been right. The next few weeks were much more peaceful, without any strange or untoward incidents taking place. But then in early November, on a weekend when Brenda was out and about with Bobby, Marcy became the target of a special message from beyond. She was in the kitchen opening up her refrigerator when several of the magnetic alphabet letters she kept on the fridge fell off. She bent over to pick them up—but when she saw the letters which remained on the refrigerator, she was shocked to her core. The remaining letters spelled out the words "DONT LEAVE ME ALONE". Just who or what was pleading with Marcy not to be left alone?

Later that evening, Marcy and Brenda got on the internet and began to do a little digging around. After numerous google searches, they finally discovered the tragic backstory of the home. The previous resident was a woman who had chained her seven-year-old foster son up in the closet—the same closet that Bobby was obsessed with—and left him there to die. The poor child's starved and dehydrated body had eventually been found by police.

Just after receiving this revelation, the sisters were startled by a rattling sound upstairs. Fearing for Bobby, they raced up to see what was causing the commotion. Upon entering the bedroom, they were shocked to find that all of the nails had been taken out of the closet door and arranged in a neat circle on the floor. Inside the closet they saw what they thought was Bobby curled up under some blankets. Without hesitation, Marcy scooped up the bundle of blankets and ran downstairs cradling it in her arms.

When she reached the living room she found Bobby himself standing before her asking, "Mommy, where are you going?" Marcy nearly screamed as she realized that whatever she was holding so close to her person was not Bobby. She let go of the blankets, and the form that had seemed solid just moments ago simply drifted away as wisps of smoke. Grabbing her son's arm, she told him, "Honey, we have to go—now!" Marcy and Bobby, with Brenda following close behind, then ran from their haunted home and never looked back.

The Haunting of Crystal Jones

Ghosts don't always just haunt houses. Sometimes they haunt people, and Crystal Jones is an excellent example of this different flavor of ghostly activity. From an early age, Crystal was quite familiar with strange ghostly happenings in the middle of the night. She actually grew up in a home that the whole family considered to be haunted. But although everyone in the house was aware of periodic strange activity, much of the phenomenon seemed to focus specifically on Crystal.

Whatever activity was following her became worse whenever she had to venture down to the basement. For Crystal, the basement always seemed to be the darkest and most frightening part of the home. She would hear voices emanating from the walls of this lower level, hushed whispers that always seemed to be talking about her. Some might suggest that these were the beginning symptoms of schizophrenia, but the voices only occurred when Crystal was in the basement. She didn't hear them anywhere else.

And the strange occurrences in the home were certainly not confined to Crystal's mind. They often found ways to physically manifest before the whole household. For example, when Crystal was about 16 years old, her grandmother passed away without a formal will, leaving the family to divvy up her belongings or throw them out. After her funeral, people simply took what they wanted for personal keepsakes.

The item that caught Crystal's eye was a painting of Jesus. She thought it was a beautiful rendering, and just staring upon the serene image gave her a feeling of peace. Deep down, she also thought that maybe having such an item in her home would help to ward off the negative entities that were conspiring to torment her. She placed the painting high up on the center of her bedroom wall.

To her horror, just a week or so later, the painting began to ooze a reddish liquid from its corners, dripping what appeared to be blood down the wall and onto the floor. Some suggested that it might be melting paint, yet the painting did not look as if it had lost any of its original paint. The strange substance continued to emanate from the edges of the painting for the next few days. Deeply disturbed and dismayed, Crystal felt she had no choice but to part with the beloved painting. She had it removed from her home.

Poltergeist activity ensued shortly thereafter, with objects moving from place to place of their own accord and lights flickering on and off by themselves. Crystal was not raised to be particularly religious, but she was so frightened by the dark forces running amuck in her house that she was naturally compelled to seek out a protective force of light to counteract the darkness. When she felt overwhelmed by the oppressive presence in her home she began to recite bible verses out loud—such as the following verse from the book of Psalms:

The Lord is my Shepherd; I shall not want. He maketh me to lie down in green pastures; he leadeth me beside still waters. He restoreth my soul; he leadeth me in the paths of righteousness for his name's sake. Yea, though I walk through the valley of the shadow of death, I will fear no evil; for thou art with me. Thy rod and thy staff—they comfort me.

She would recite this verse over and over until she felt relief from the sinister presence that inhabited her home. But the entities in the home did not take too kindly to her recitations from the Holy Bible, and they began to make their displeasure known. She would routinely wake up with unexplained scratches on her body. And in one of the scariest incidents, she woke up to see a clock running backwards and three figures clad head to toe in all black standing in her room.

Such night terrors were too much for her to take, and as soon as she was able, she moved out. At the tender age of 18, shortly after graduating high school, she found a full-time job and moved into a shared apartment with a few friends. Crystal thought she had left the horrors of her childhood behind, but she was mistaken. Shortly after she moved into the apartment, strange and disturbing things again began to occur, and once again Crystal was the focal point.

The activity began in the crudest of fashions. Crystal woke up to find what appeared to be feces smeared on the wall. There are several accounts of hauntings in which biological material such as urine, feces, or blood physically manifested itself on the surroundings. Such incidents are generally ascribed to something more powerful and insidious than the average ghost.

In theory, the souls of the dearly departed don't leave these kinds of calling cards—they can only come from forces of a more demonic nature.

This is precisely what Crystal and her frightened roommates deduced. The others encouraged Crystal to go to the local Catholic church to be prayed for. Figuring she had nothing left to lose, she agreed. That night she went to a "healing service" and had several church members pray for her to be delivered. According to Crystal, the second the priest laid eyes on her, he realized that something really terrible was following her around.

The priest immediately laid hands on her in an effort to exorcise the evil from her person. But as soon as he began praying, Crystal began levitating off the ground! Defying the laws of physics, she slowly rose into the air before crashing back down on the church floor. She began screaming uncontrollably as the clergy sought to restrain her. The priest then poured holy water over her head and face. The water burned her flesh, which according to Catholic lore is an indication that holy water is "working".

Wasting to time, the priest then went ahead and began the rites of exorcism to expel the unclean spirit. He spoke over Crystal in authoritative Latin, speaking the special phrases of exorcism that are as old as the Catholic Church itself. According to witnesses, Crystal began to speak in a demonic voice, indicating that the evil presence was indeed inside of her. After several hours, Crystal was truly delivered. She finally felt victorious over the evil entities, and as she returned to the now quite pleasant surroundings of her new apartment, she felt that she had been granted a new lease on life.

Frightening Visions

After her husband passed away, Regina Thompson lived a quiet life, devoting most of her time to raising her five-year-old son Markus. Over the next few years it was just the two of them living and struggling through life together. When Markus was about eight years old they moved into a small rental house. It was a rather modest abode, but it was within the single mother's budget, and not far from the neighborhood where she herself had grown up.

Wishing to reconnect with her roots, she readily signed the lease. She thought that this humble little home was just the new start that she and her son needed, but her peace of mind was shattered on the very first night when she woke up from a horrible dream. It wasn't just a nightmare, it seemed more like a memory—not *her* memory, but some kind of conscious recollection that had been somehow downloaded into her mind from somewhere else.

In the dream she found herself at the site of a grisly crime scene. From her vantage point, she could see the dead body of a girl slumped over the side of a bathtub with her head cut off. Her freshly chopped neck was still spurting blood and her body was quickly taking on a bluish cast from lack of oxygen. The mortal remains of this girl were folded right over the side of the tub as if someone had forced her into position and used the side of the bathtub as an improvised chopping block.

Upon seeing this nightmarish vision of horrendous homicide, Regina opened her eyes, screaming herself awake. Such dreams were by no means normal for Regina. In all of her life she had never had such a shockingly realistic dream of violence and death. She had never dreamed anything close to such carnage before, so why now? She was not a fan of horror novels, she didn't watch gory movies, and if violence came up on the nightly newscast she would quickly change the channel.

Regina was not someone who entertained such thoughts, so where did these dreams of brutality come from? The fact that this disturbing dream was some sort of foreign intrusion upon her consciousness became clear in the following days as the dream became a recurring nightmare. Every single night she would dream the same awful dream, seeing the same horrible vision of the bathtub decapitation victim. And these haunted night visions would soon express themselves during the daytime hours as well.

One morning she went to the bathroom to get ready and found that her towel rack had been knocked to the ground. At first, she didn't think too much of it, telling herself that it must have been a freak accident. She supposed that the rack must have just come loose and gravity did the rest, so she simply put her stuff away and went about her day. But later that afternoon she was relaxing in front of her television set when another seemingly stable structure somehow launched itself right off of its bearings. One of the pot racks on the kitchen wall had abruptly flung itself down to the ground, seemingly of its own volition.

Needless to say, this incident, combined with her recurring nightmares, really gave Regina the creeps. The next day she caught sight of her downstairs neighbor and questioned her a bit about the history of the house. The woman gave Regina an earful. According to her, several previous tenants had broken their leases, all complaining of strange activity in the upstairs apartment.

Now Regina pretty much knew beyond a shadow of a doubt that something was haunting her home. The next incident happened when Regina's doorbell rang just before midnight. Regina was a homebody who turned in early, and she certainly was not expecting any company at that late hour, so she was automatically unnerved. Part of her wondered if her downstairs neighbor was back to report more oddities about the rental home, but this was not the case. As she looked through the peephole of her door, she didn't see her neighbor—she didn't see anyone. Against her better judgment, she opened the door and looked up and down the hallway outside her apartment. There was no on there.

Fed up with such antics, Regina sought out a medium the very next day in an attempt to get to the bottom of the intrusion. The medium immediately sensed that there was indeed a spirit in the apartment. She also felt a strong impression that the spirit that inhabited the home was somehow connected to a nearby intersection or crosswalk.

As soon as the medium mentioned this, Regina's mind immediately went to the train tracks that were situated behind her home. She remembered something that she had heard a few years before—a bit of tragic news that she had mostly forgotten about. An old friend of hers from high school named Kathy Green had been walking along those very tracks when she was hit and killed by a train. Tragically, the blow she received was so powerful that she was decapitated upon impact.

The community in which Regina grew up was very close-knit, and any sudden death of a young person—especially one so brutal and tragic—was immediately the talk of the town. And as it turned out, Kathy was even a distant relative of her son, on his father's side. When Regina informed the medium of these details, the clairvoyant nodded in recognition, as if it all now made sense.

The medium then opened a dialogue with the earthbound spirit of her former classmate and discovered that Kathy was still haunting this plane of existence because she was afraid of what might lie in store for her on the other side. You see, Kathy had made a lot of mistakes in her life, and she was deeply afraid that she would be punished for them in the afterlife. It was this fear that was keeping her from "going to the light". However, the medium was able to convince Kathy that she had nothing to fear and help her to finally pass on in peace.

But even though Kathy had been helped on toward her destiny in the afterlife, the haunting activity continued. In the following days, Regina would awaken to pounding and banging sounds all throughout her apartment. Thoroughly freaked out, she had the same medium make a house call.

It was then that the medium informed her that Kathy had served as a cover hiding a much darker force. This entity was full of pure negative energy, with murderous intent. Unfortunately, this acknowledgement of the entity's presence only served to increase the intensity of its attacks. Doors began slamming shut, and a shadowy figure even began appearing from time to time in dark corners and doorways.

Above all else, Regina and her son felt like they were being watched at all times by something with malevolent intentions. Regina now believed that Kathy's spirit had actually been protecting them from whatever else was lurking in the background.

The medium was soon called back for round three with the entity, and this time she was able to sense that what they were dealing with was not human. In her mind's eye she could see a big dark figure with wings, almost like a dragon, take shape. The entity was sucking all the life out of the immediate vicinity, growing bigger and stronger from the fear it provoked. The medium believed that this was the real reason behind all of Regina's hellish nightmares: They were a means for the being to extract the greatest amount of fear from her. Realizing that they were dealing with something beyond human capacity, the medium—though not a practicing Christian—turned to God and prayed for him to send down his angels to get rid of the demon.

The medium claims that she then witnessed a titanic battle ensue as archangels descended right through the ceiling and confronted the nebulous beast. Two massive angels each grabbed hold of the dark entity and ejected it from the apartment. The angels, with their task apparently finished, then flew back up through the ceiling from whence they had come.

The medium, who is the only one to have seen this titanic struggle firsthand, admits that the culmination of Regina's haunting sounds way too fantastic—even for a ghost story—for most to believe. But she stands by her report. And as for Regina and her son? Since this supposed angelic intervention, they have had no further problems and have been able to rest soundly.

Ghost Hunter Becomes Ghost Hunted

In the early 2000s ghost hunting was all the rage, with TV shows on the subject popping up on every channel. The most popular of these was the infamous *Ghost Hunters*, in which a group of average Joes—plumbers by day, paranormal investigators by night—traveled across the country to investigate alleged hauntings.

Mark Davis, minus the fame and a primetime TV show, was just such a freelance paranormal investigator. His trouble started when he was investigating a demonic-style haunting at a historic old home in New England. Mark's work had spread awareness about what was going on at the site, and he would later theorize that the entities themselves took umbrage to this spotlight and sought to strike out at him where he was the most vulnerable—his family back home.

Incredibly, even while Mark and a camera crew were filming an area supposedly haunted by a menacing shadow-figure, his son Paul several miles away would encounter the very same being. Paul was simply taking out the trash when he received the shock of his life. After tossing a trash bag into the trashcan outside, he noticed something dark out of the corner of his eye. He turned to see what can only be described as a "living shadow". It was in the form of a man, yet dark from head to toe.

Scared to death at what he saw, Paul immediately ran inside and called his father up on the telephone to describe the incident. Hearing the fear in his son's voice, Mark wanted to drop everything, ditch his current investigation and head on home. But he was too involved to just bail on everyone who was depending on him, so with a heavy heart he told his son to "hang in there" and said he would be home soon.

Back home, Paul decided to crash out on the couch with the lights on and the TV blaring, but even these psychological comforts were not enough to put his mind at ease. Finally, he tried to go to sleep, but he was soon woken up by odd noises. When he opened his eyes, he saw what he thought was one of his father's decorative figurines—a three-inch tall African tribesman he'd picked up in Kenya—walking across the table. Thoroughly spooked, Paul ended up staying awake the rest of the night, nervously looking about the room for any further signs of disturbance.

Mark came home the next morning and began to go through his routine process of investigation—except this time with his own home. At first, he was thoroughly stumped. He didn't pick up any obvious signals that there was a haunting in his home. You see, Mark is not exactly a medium, but he is an intuitive who can "feel" the presence of spirits more readily than most. But when Mark concentrated his senses in the immediate area, he didn't feel any negative spirits. He actually just picked up a happy, warm, and pleasant vibe, one that you would associate with a loving, caring home.

This would soon prove to be nothing but a clever facade, however, because later that evening the entity emerged and began attacking Paul all over again. The family was at the dinner table when Paul began to complain of an intense pressure in his chest. Then something struck him across the side of the face just as he was putting a spoonful of mashed potatoes in his mouth. It was as if something had smacked him upside the head with a ferocious fury. Everyone at the table heard the sound of the blow and saw the force with which Paul's head was jerked to the side. They also saw the accompanying red mark presenting itself as physical proof of a literal "unseen hand" at work.

Bearing witness to this, Mark began to seriously consider whether the same entities that he has spent his career hunting were now hunting him and his family. Not wanting to allow the dark entities to gather any further strength, Mark decided to conduct an exorcism of the house immediately. He began burning incense and chanting prayers in the home. It seemed to work, and soon the malicious beings dissipated from their waking environment. His son Paul was immensely grateful for the relief, and Mark the ghost hunter learned a very valuable lesson—he learned the importance of not taking his work home with him!

A Haunting in Connecticut

The story of the Snedekers' haunted home in Connecticut has really made the rounds in recent decades, even becoming fodder for big-budget Hollywood movies. But what really happened in Al and Carmen Snedeker's house?

The story begins with the Snedekers seeking out an affordable home in Southington, Connecticut, in order to be closer to the medical center where their son was being treated for Hodgkin's Lymphoma. The family, which was already strapped for cash due to the ongoing medical expenses, jumped at the chance when they were shown a large house that was within their budget. But this seemingly ideal home quickly proved otherwise.

On the very day they moved in, Al found some rather strange artifacts in the basement. He discovered what looked like an embalming table and embalming tools. Shortly after this startling discovery, the family's worst fears were confirmed: their dream home used to be a funeral home.

But they had already unpacked, and in any event it was too late for them to back out of the deal now. The Snedekers tried to put the house's past out of their minds and focus on the present, but shades of the home's history were not so easily put to rest.

First, Carmen began to hear strange sounds emanating from various parts of the home. She also noticed that certain household items would inexplicably disappear only to reappear days later in unusual places. Other members of the family began to report even more distinct manifestations, such as disembodied voices speaking to them and even shadowy people moving about just at the edge of their vision.

But it was their eldest son who seemed most affected. Life for young Philip Snedeker had been hard already as he dealt with his cancer treatments, and now whatever it was that he was encountering in the home was enough to send him right over the edge.

Shortly after moving in, Philip had the strange sensation that he was being watched. He also began hearing a faint whisper that seemed to be calling his name. He informed his mother of these strange experiences shortly after their arrival, but she brushed them off as just his imagination. Realizing that no one would take his claims seriously, he became much quieter than usual and purposefully isolated himself from friends and family. And when Philip did talk, the things he said were unsettling. He described a strange figure with long black hair who would come to visit him at night. He also claimed this figure spoke to him.

But it wasn't only Philip who saw strange visitors. Soon the other Snedeker children were seeing things as well. On one occasion they told Al that they had seen four men in dark cloaks in the basement. The distress in their voices was so real that their dad felt he had to believe them. However, he wasn't thinking that they were being beset by ghosts; his gut reaction was that someone had broken into the home. Al was a gruff, no-nonsense fighter, perfectly capable of handling himself. He headed downstairs with a flashlight, wanting to protect his family and determined to teach whoever it was a lesson they wouldn't soon forget. But he found the basement completely empty. No one was there.

The Snedekers then held a family meeting to reason with their fearful children. They tried to convince them that there was no intruder, that it was just their imaginations working overtime. They also singled out Philip for stirring up the younger children's fears by telling them he was seeing things.

Philip naturally resented his parents' lack of belief and their attempt to pin blame on him, and his angst now turned into open hostility. He often wrote disturbing things in a personal notebook, reflecting on death and destruction. A cousin of his named Tammy became concerned. She wondered why he wrote such things—and she also wondered how he *could* write such things when he was severely dyslexic. When she asked Philip, he stated that "the man helped me write them".

His behavior then took a turn for the worse as he became aggressive and began to strike out at his relatives—including the selfsame cousin who had become perhaps just a bit too curious about his notebook. This incident finally convinced his family to take proactive measures. They sent Philip in for an evaluation which resulted in a diagnosis of schizophrenia.

From the standpoint of psychiatric professionals, this was the only logical diagnosis. Upon learning that Philip was seeing apparitions and hearing voices, they immediately assumed the young man had lost his mind. They absolutely refused to entertain the possibility that he was experiencing anything paranormal.

Philip was removed from the home shortly thereafter, but the malicious activity didn't stop. In fact, it became worse. It seems that the entities had been focusing on Philip, and in his absence they turned their attention to Carmen and her niece Tammy and began a vicious campaign of the worst possible abuse imaginable.

Both women began to experience routine sexual assaults by unseen attackers. Al was enraged to hear such reports and felt powerless to protect his family—and to make matters even worse, Al himself soon became a victim of these selfsame assaults. Yes, the sexually deviant spirits were apparently equal opportunity rapists, and on several occasions Al too was sodomized by unseen forces.

Carmen also began to see the same strange entity that Philip had seen—the tall black shape that had appeared to him in the middle of the night. These sexual assaults and startling visions showed her just how wrong she had been not to believe her son's stories of encounters with the paranormal. Having exhausted all rational explanations, the Snedekers called their local Catholic church to request that a priest come to their home the following day to conduct an exorcism.

The spirits in the home must have been listening in on that phone call, though. The next morning, Carmen became the victim of what was apparently a targeted assassination attempt. She taking a shower before the priest arrived when the shower curtains suddenly moved of their own volition and wrapped tightly around her face, cutting off her air supply and beginning to smother her. She struggled with all of her might and was finally she was able to break free enough to scream for help.

Tammy heard her and came running to the rescue. Upon entering the bathroom, she saw the bizarre sight of the shower curtain seemingly coming to life to murder her aunt. Desperate to save her, Tammy pulled and struggled against the curtain until sections of it finally ripped away and Carmen was able to break free.

The house was indeed eventually exorcised of its demons, and the family managed to live there in peace for two more years. Nevertheless, they were none to sorry to leave when they finally did move out.

Evil Hangers-on

Katherine Smith had never believed in ghosts or spirits, but that changed when an old friend named Margaret dropped by for a visit. As they were catching up, Margaret, who was obviously disturbed, opened up to her friend about her troubled life. Since she'd last seen Katherine, she had met a man, gotten married, and gotten pregnant. That was all happy news—but then her husband had made a startling confession.

He had joined a cult either just before or just after their marriage. This was alarming enough, but his next admission would make anyone's blood run cold. This cult routinely conducted human sacrifices, and he had agreed to offer up his first-born son as one of the group's sacrificial lambs. Margaret was obviously terrified by what her husband had told her, but as shocking as the story was, Katherine the skeptic was not completely convinced that it was true. She figured that Margaret's husband was simply playing some sort of demented, cruel, and sadistic prank upon the gullible young woman. Katherine gave Margaret a few comforting words and sent her troubled friend on her way.

But a year later, Margaret returned with an even more disturbing story. She now claimed that her husband had been brutally murdered by the same occult group that had been targeting her son. Cult members had ambushed him, slit his wrists and throat, and left him to bleed to death in a field on the edge of town. To her, it was obvious that his death was murder, yet the county coroner had ruled it a suicide.

Margaret also claimed that the cult was continuing to follow and harass her. She said that they left threatening messages and made threatening phone calls, telling her that they "owned her" and that the baby was theirs. Appalled at what she was hearing, Katherine agreed to let Margaret stay with her for a while. But this act of kindness would prove to be the biggest mistake of her life. Because by inviting her friend into her home, she also invited all of her problems.

Soon she too was beset by all manner of strange phenomena. The first thing she noticed was objects being rearranged on their own, which is a classic sign of haunting that is repeated in many alleged cases. Experts contend that this is the initial "welcoming" by the spirits. They start out slow, simply moving items around to get your attention, and then once they have it, they intensify their activity.

Katherine would wake up to find her kids' toys strewn all over the floor. Messy kids, of course, aren't exactly a paranormal phenomenon per se, but after Katherine reprimanded her children several times and they always adamantly protested that they were not the culprits, she began to realize that something else was going on. This was confirmed when pictures suddenly began dropping from the walls, many of them smashing and breaking. Even one of Katherine's wedding photos was shattered on the ground.

Feeling increasingly uneasy with the strange activity in her house, Katherine told Margaret that she had to go. But when Margaret left, the negative entity that had arrived with her decided to stay.

Shortly after Margaret's eviction, Katherine was doing dishes when she suddenly felt a cold wind and smelled a horrible rotting smell. She glanced over at the nearby window thinking that someone had left it open, but the window was closed with the blinds drawn. The next thing she knew, she felt strong arms wrap around her and someone grinding obscenely against her rear end. This decidedly rude interruption to an evening of peaceful dishwashing only lasted for about 30 seconds, but Katherine felt understandably violated. And even worse than the violation was the terror of not knowing who or what had perpetrated it.

No one had broken into her home to assault her; there was no serial molester on the prowl. Just how do you report an invisible entity to the police? As she sat on her couch shaking in fear, waiting for her husband, James, to get home, Katherine began to consider that perhaps she was losing her mind. Maybe it was all in her head—a hallucination?

But when her husband came home and managed to get bits and pieces of the awful story out of his wife, he took her to the bathroom and examined her arms where she said she had felt someone pinning them tightly to her side. Shockingly, he found huge bruises all up and down her arms—bruises such as you might find after someone held you in a death-grip.

Feeling nauseated with disgust and sick with fear, Katherine said she wanted to wash up and take a bath. Her worried husband obligingly left the room. Alone in the bath, Katherine ran the hot water over her body hoping that she could just forget the whole thing. But even as she was trying to wash away what had happened, she felt the palm of someone's hand press down on the top of her head. The hand forcefully shoved her head down into the water. It was only a few seconds before the hand released its pressure, but Katherine thought she was going to die. Pulling her head up and gasping for air, she looked around for her assailant, but of course there was no one there. She quickly jumped out of the bathtub, wrapped a towel around herself, and in a voice quivering with fear, told her husband, "James, I don't want to die—we have to leave!"

But picking up and moving out was easier said than done—and besides, Katherine didn't know if moving would solve anything. For all she knew, the entity would just follow her. She felt like she was stuck. She was completely terrified, but she didn't know what to do.

Katherine was still in the middle of this terrible quandary when the entity decided to introduce itself visibly. Late one night, she was up watching television while her children were in bed and her husband was still at work. As she stared at the TV screen she saw movement out of the corner of her eye. She glanced toward the door to the hallway and saw a dark figure. The being was pure black, just a shadowy form, but it seemed that its head was turned directly toward her, staring at her.

Katherine was completely consumed with terror, but the only words that escaped from her mouth were a quiet "No—no!" Suddenly, the being rushed at her as if it were going to leap upon her. Closing her eyes, she feebly raised her hands to fend off the attack But as she waited for the worst, nothing happened. She opened her eyes and the entity was gone as if it had never been there in the first place.

Understandably shaken, Katherine asked her mother to stay with her for a while. However, the dark being simply ignored the chaperone and soon began abusing Katherine right in front of her mom's eyes. The two were sitting on the couch chatting one evening when something seemed to grab Katherine by the arm and throw her off the couch. Her mother instantly became a believer that something was very wrong with the house, and she ordered her daughter to take the kids and leave.

But Katherine had another idea. She intuitively realized that the entity was targeting her personally, and the best way to protect her kids at this point was to get them as far away from her as she could. So, with tears in her eyes, she pleaded for her mother to take her kids to her home and keep them there where they would be safe from the ghostly attacks against her.

Reluctantly, her mother agreed, gathered up the kids, and went back to her home. While her kids were safely away, Katherine resolved to get to the bottom of the phenomenon. She called up the one who she saw as the source of all her recent misery, her old friend Margaret, and asked her to come over. When Margaret arrived, Katherine told her what was happening—and was shocked by her lack of compassion when she bluntly retorted, "So? That's your problem now!"

At this point, Katherine flatly denounced Margaret and told her that she never wanted to see her again. And incredibly, this emotional rejection of Margaret seemed to reject the evil entity as well. Now that Margaret was banished for good, so was her evil hanger-on.

Some experts theorize that negative energy may occasionally work through negative people. If this was the case here, then closing off the source from which the dark entity sprung—Margaret herself—would have an effective means of shutting out the entity.

As for Katherine Smith, she has never claimed to be an expert on the mechanics underpinning the paranormal—but she has not had any problems since.

Demonic Attacks in the French Quarter

According to local residents, the old home on the corner of 20217 Fairway Drive in Springfield, Louisiana, is haunted. And not just by any run-of-the-mill ghost—this house is said to be haunted by some of the evilest and most malevolent entities you could ever come into contact with.

Just ask Jean Bartoli her opinion on the matter, and she will give you an earful. She and her husband, Andy, bought the place in the summer of 2014 thinking it was a great find. The house was old and in need of some renovation, but she figured it wasn't anything that she and her husband couldn't handle. But the renovation needed on this old structure was more than met the eye. Besides new insulation and wood paneling, this haunted house was in need of a complete spiritual makeover.

The Bartolis did not move into the house right away. Instead they parked an RV in the yard so they could live in it while they made the necessary renovations. It wasn't spacious, but they figured it was good enough for the time being.

Once they began renovating the house, Jean was the first to experience the dark spirits that haunted it. Andy was still working outside when she decided to start painting the interior. She cranked up the stereo to keep herself in a good mood as she painted, but out of nowhere the radio died. She put her paintbrush down and went over to inspect the radio. The plug was still in the outlet, and as far as she could tell the power hadn't gone out, yet the radio had inexplicably powered off. Not sure what could have caused it, she turned it back on.

But as soon as she picked up her paintbrush and resumed her work, the radio turned off once again. And upon inspection she once again found it to be plugged in, with full power. There was just no logical explanation as to how the radio could have died like that. Still, it wasn't a big deal. Jean forgot about the whole thing and moved on with the renovations and planning for her son Jonathan's upcoming birthday.

On the day of the big birthday bash she made sure everything was in order. Jonathan's little friends were there and the party games were all lined up. But there weren't enough refreshments, so Jean had to make a last-minute run to the store to get some soda. No problem; her mom was there to watch the kids, and she would only be gone for a few minutes.

When she got back less than half an hour later, however, everything had changed. She found her mother sitting outside with a horrified expression on her face. She asked her what was wrong, and she cried out, "You've got something in your house!" While Jean had been gone, some entity had apparently manifested to her mother in the form of footsteps, scraping, and distant whispers. Her mother was so frightened that she refused to set foot in her own daughter's house ever again.

When Jean later told Andy about her mom's reaction, he wasn't concerned. "Jean, look—your mom just watches way too many scary movies and TV shows. That's all."

Jean hoped that Andy's facile explanation was right, but deep down she knew that it was wrong. And soon thereafter her suspicions were confirmed when she was by herself washing dishes in the house's kitchen. You see, although the family were not yet sleeping in the home, they took their meals there instead of inside the cramped RV. So it was that Jean was cleaning up after dinner when the entity made itself known. As she was washing the dishes, she felt a cold wind brush through her hair. The windows were shut, and it wasn't even windy outside, so the phenomenon immediately seemed odd.

It wasn't threatening, though, so she simply shrugged and went back to the task at hand. But she had barely washed and dried another dish before she was disturbed again, this time by the sensation that something had tapped her right on the shoulder—which should have been impossible. Andy was still at work, and her mother had just picked up the kids and taken them to her house for the evening. Jean should have been completely alone, yet someone had tapped her shoulder.

Summoning her courage, she turned around in absolute terror to see who was behind her. But again, there was no one to be seen. Even as she turned to examine her surroundings in the kitchen, she was horrified to feel someone grab her ponytail and yank it in the other direction. This was enough for Jean. She bolted right out of the kitchen and ran straight to the RV parked outside.

She was immensely relieved when Andy came home, but she was not reassured when he insisted that what she claimed to have experienced was simply not possible. Andy absolutely refused to entertain the possibility that something paranormal was occurring in the home.

Jean's distress at the strange happenings soon grew worse when the malevolent spirits began targeting Jonathan. She and the boy were alone in the house one afternoon when she noticed him talking to himself. She listened more closely, and he seemed to be having a whole conversation. Growing concerned, she asked him, "What are you doing?"

He replied, "Just talking with this guy." He motioned to the corner to indicate whoever he was talking to, but Jean didn't see anyone there.

"What guy, buddy? Who's talking to you? I don't see anyone." But Jonathan insisted that there was indeed someone lurking in the corner and carrying on a conversation with him. Realizing that it was pointless to argue with her toddler, Jean decided to play along and asked him, "OK… well, then, what are you guys talking about?"

The child then coldly looked up at his mother and shouted, "About how you should all die!"

The little boy had never before shown any predilection toward violence, much less violence directed toward his own mother. Somehow this evil presence was now using him as a mouthpiece to voice these evil intentions. Jean was horrified to say the least. Picking up Jonathan, she took him outside to the RV in an attempt to end the conversation he was having with whatever entity lurked inside that haunted home.

Terror stricken and with hours to wait before Andy got home, Jean called up her dad to tell him what was going on. Her father didn't understand what he was hearing, but he immediately recognized the fear in her voice and sprang into action. He rushed to the property, and Jean invited him into the RV to discuss what they should do next. Jean did not want to go back into the house, but her father insisted upon accompanying inside her to "check it out".

They were looking around and making sure that nothing was amiss when Jean's father noticed a rosary necklace hanging from the attic door. As they looked at it, it began to sway back and forth of its own volition and a strong, cold wind began blowing through the home. The two were then startled by a loud thump coming from directly above them in the attic. Seconds later, another loud banging sound reverberated overhead.

Jean was now inconsolably frightened, but her father chose to give in to anger rather than fear. He screamed a challenge at the entity, shouting, "You son of a bitch! Who are you? Answer me! Who are you? Go ahead and come out, damn you!"

The entity did not visibly reveal itself, however. Instead, it began assaulting Jean right in front of her helpless father. She felt a burning sensation in the middle of her back and cried out as she felt claws digging into her flesh. She lifted up her shirt to find three fresh, bleeding cuts on her back. Not wishing to provoke any further violence against his daughter, her now much more subdued father led Jean out of the house.

They waited inside the RV until Andy came home and then told him what had occurred. Much to Jean's chagrin, however, Andy still refused to believe that the house was haunted. To the outrage of both his wife and father-in-law, Andy basically insinuated that they were just making the whole thing up. It was obvious that Andy simply would not believe it unless he saw the activity with his own two eyes—and he would soon be granted that opportunity.

As he led his perturbed family members back into the house, he continued to expound about how ridiculous they were being—until the bathroom door suddenly slammed in his face. Not softly, but loudly and forcefully. Andy then stared in disbelief as the doorknob slowly turned by itself and the door opened before slamming shut once again.

Stunned, Andy stepped back, and the man who'd been insisting just seconds before that "ghosts don't exist" quietly told his wife, "Honey, I think we might need an exorcist." The previously unbelieving Andy then expressed his newfound acceptance of the reality of the supernatural by methodically placing crosses all over the home in an attempt to ward off the evil spirits.

Jean, taking a page from the very same ghost shows that Andy had previously ridiculed, left a small recording device on the kitchen table and hit the RECORD button. She wanted to capture an EVP to see whether any disembodied voices would appear on the tape. And she wasn't disappointed. When the family took the device back to their RV later and hit the PLAY button, they could hear unearthly grunts, groans and growls.

Even worse, towards the end of the recording, these guttural noises managed to form words. A voice could clearly be heard shouting, "They will all die!" Insidious laughter followed this evil proclamation, and then the recording ended. It was as if the entities knew they were being recorded and were waiting until the very end of the tape to issue this shocking message.

After hearing this, Jean's first inclination was to get her family as far from that demon-haunted house as fast as she possibly could. As is often the case, however, it just wasn't that easy.

The family had practically gone broke buying the property, and if they just up and left they would be financially ruined. They felt like they were stuck. They didn't know how they could stay, but they had nowhere else to go, so they continued their limbo existence of living in a camper in the yard, just outside the hellish house that was tormenting them.

The demons that ruled the roost interrupted this unstable equilibrium soon enough, however, when they reached out to inflict harm on Jean's son. She was outside watching the boy play when he managed to escape her supervision. She had looked away for just a minute or so, but as all parents know, one minute is all it takes for a child to wander off. Not seeing where he'd gone, Jean immediately jumped up to find him. She then heard him laughing up above her. To her horror she looked up to see Jonathan in the upstairs window. He had run into the house!

She yelled at him, "Jonathan! Jonathan! Come down! Come back!" But the child just continued to play, completely oblivious to his terror-stricken mother. Jean took a deep breath. She knew she had to go inside to get him, yet deep down she somehow also knew that it was a trap. She could feel it in her soul. She was sure that these dastardly demons were using her own son as bait to lure her back into that hateful house.

But there was nothing she could do about it. Andy was at work and she was the only one there to go get Jonathan. And so, trying her best to control her fear, she walked up to the front door and stepped inside. Not wanting to remain inside any longer than necessary, she practically ran up the stairs to the room where she had just seen Jonathan. But the room was now empty. She turned around to leave, but her exit was blocked. As she tried to pass through the doorway, she collided with some kind of invisible wall. She could still see out of the doorway, but it was as if a sheet of clear glass had materialized over the exit and she could not cross the threshold.

As terrifying as this phenomenon was, things got scarier as she was suddenly lifted up into the air and slammed down onto the floor face first. She then saw a swirling black mass emerge in the corner of the room. This shadowy mist coalesced into the form of a man who jumped onto her back. Straddling her prostrate form, the being began to strangle her as it screamed, "What's underneath the carpet? Take a look under the carpet!"

Jean found her hands involuntarily following these instructions, and she began to pull up pieces of carpet, revealing the occult symbols that had been etched into the hardwood underneath. She could see a giant pentagram and other arcane artwork staining the surface. Once she uncovered the occult symbols, the entity released her and faded back into the ether.

Now free to move, Jean jumped up and—temporarily forgetting all about Jonathan—ran right out the door and into her RV. To her immense relief, Jonathan was there waiting for her. It now seemed likely to her that Jonathan had never been in the house to begin with, and that the demon had simply projected his image into the upstairs window in order to lure her into going inside.

Now that she had uncovered clear evidence of occult practices being carried out in the house, she also wondered what these demonic entities wanted. Hoping to find some answers, she called up a priest (these stories always seem to end with a priest!) and requested him to come and bless the house. The priest readily agreed to perform this routine task, but upon his arrival he instantly sensed that there were demons in the house. He began walking through every room, chanting and praying for the demonic spirits to leave.

As this was going on, Jean and Andy were waiting in the kitchen. Suddenly, Jean became physically ill. Andy had her sit down at the kitchen table to rest, but she only seemed to get worse. Jean later stated that she felt that she was under direct attack by one of the demonic entities, and that it was literally attempting to possess her. She lost all sense of control and awareness, feeling as if she had fallen into some sort of "outer darkness" far away from everyone and everything.

Even as Jean was facing off against these inner demons, the priest stepped into the kitchen to declare that the evil entities had been banished. Andy thanked him, walked him to the door, and bid him goodbye. He hoped and prayed that the demons were truly gone—but the reality was a little more complicated than that. According to Jean's later testimony, during the blessing ritual, one of the demons managed to avoid banishment by hiding inside of her and physically possessing her.

Her possession became clear to Andy when Jean and he were on their way to pick up their kids from their grandparents' house. For most of the drive Jean was unresponsive and staring blankly ahead. And when Andy finally got his wife to look at him and make eye contact, a chill went down his spine. Just by seeing the darkness in her eyes, he knew that there was something seriously wrong with his wife. Jean's parents quickly realized this too, and when her father asked her what was wrong, Jean's face contorted in rage as she barked, "You better back up, old man! Just back the f—k up!"

If they needed any further evidence that Jean was "not herself", then this was the smoking gun. Jean loved her father and had nothing but respect for him. Never in her wildest dreams would she have spoken to him in such a manner. Not knowing what else to do, Jean's frightened relatives placed another call to the priest, who arrived within the hour and quickly administered the rite of exorcism to expel the demon that was apparently hiding within Jean's mortal coil.

Jean's disposition changed immediately. As if waking from a coma, she looked around in confusion asking, "What? Where am I? What happened?" And to the amazement of everyone present, a swirling black mass climbed up over her head. The nebulous cloud drifted up to the ceiling, where it dissipated and vanished from sight.

This additional exorcism apparently banished the last lingering demon for good. But even so, this family soon found another place to live.

The New Ghost in Town

Jesse Smith was a hardworking young man who spent his days toiling away in a rubber factory in Fort Wayne, Indiana. And as hard as he worked during the day, he played just as hard at night. A fan of fine spirits (of the strictly alcoholic kind), he haunted the bars, taverns, and house parties of northeastern Indiana. It was at one of the latter that he met the love of his life, a young woman named Maria Alvarado.

He was enamored with Maria from the beginning, and their relationship started off strong. There was only one problem: This girl who habitually visited the party scene in Fort Wayne actually lived about 25 miles away, just outside of Huntington. Their long-distance relationship sufficed for a start, but as things progressed Jesse wanted to close that gap. He didn't have any plan, or any job lined up, but like the brave, intrepid soul he was, he just went for it.

So taking up Maria's mother's offer to stay at their home until he got on his feet, the tenacious young man eventually found a job and an apartment of his own nearby. It was an old farmhouse that had been converted into a duplex. It wasn't in the best of shape, but Jesse figured that it was good enough.

The first signs of the paranormal occurred during a housewarming party Jesse threw for his and Maria's social circle. Toward the end of the festivities Jesse and Maria excused themselves for the night, but they invited their guests to stay and party on. And right when the couple were in the middle of—let's just say, an intimate moment—they heard a pounding on their bedroom door. But this was no ghost, it was Jesse's old high school buddy Todd Miller. Jesse, somewhat displeased to be interrupted, didn't mince words as he shouted, "Todd! What the hell do you want?!?"

Todd was obviously drunk, as his stumbling gait and slurred words indicated, but one look at his bleeding leg was enough to sober them both up. His entire lower leg was covered in blood. Jesse's eyes widened as he exclaimed, "What the hell happened to your leg?"

Todd stuttered, "Do—don't know, dude. I was just chilling upstairs downing a 40-ounce one minute—and the next thing I know something is cutting into me like a knife!"

"What?!? Who cut you?" Jesse demanded.

But Todd was dumbfounded as he raised his hands in exasperation and exclaimed, "Dude I don't know! I was sitting up in the attic by myself!"

"By yourself?" Jesse echoed.

"Yes!" Todd affirmed. "And all of a sudden it was like some invisible hand slashed my leg with a knife!"

The next day, Jesse and a couple of his buddies went up to explore the attic. His first theory was that there must be raccoons or squirrels up in the attic and maybe one had bitten Todd and retreated into the darkness before he could see it. So he armed himself with his megawatt flashlight and a broom, determined to drive the critters out. But the attic was completely deserted. There were no animals, and no sign of any animals anywhere to be seen. Nor were there any sharp objects that Todd might have bumped into or fallen on.

But while the cause of Todd's injury remained a mystery, the group did find one new and mysterious piece of the puzzle. On a milk crate in the corner there was a stack of paperwork. Jesse had never noticed it before. Upon looking at the papers, he was amazed to find the blueprints for a church. He hadn't known that an architect had lived in this building. Who had created these designs and what were they for?

After wrapping up his inspection of the attic, he bought the papers back down with him and set them on the coffee table in the living room, planning to examine them in more detail when he got back from work. But upon his return he found the blueprints completely shredded by his mischievous Boston Terrier, who seemed to have had a bad case of separation anxiety—separation anxiety no doubt exacerbated by ghostly activity—while his owner was away.

And as soon as that batch of blueprints was destroyed, the haunting of Jesse's duplex was fully unleashed. In the following days there was a heavy, oppressive feel all throughout the apartment. Then one night, Jesse and Maria were sitting on the couch relaxing and watching TV when they heard a loud boom from the ceiling above them. According to Jesse, that boom sounded like a bomb going off, and they both immediately jumped up if the house was under attack.

They then clearly heard what sounded like something being dragged across the attic floor above them. Maria looked over at Jesse in shock and quietly asked, "Is it the raccoons again?"

Knowing full well how impossible it was that the racket they'd just heard had been caused by animals, Jesse snorted, "Yeah, right! Maybe if a raccoon was dropped from a helicopter, crashed through the roof, and had its dead body dragged across the attic floor. Yeah! Maybe it was a raccoon!"

For the rest of the week there were periodic odd occurrences such as items being moved or outright disappearing. There were also random cold spots which would be freezing cold even during the full heat of the afternoon sun. Along with these strange physical manifestations, there were also psychological changes among the people living in the house. Many residents became noticeably more anxious and agitated. Jesse himself began to get into more arguments. There were even several fights over petty household issues like "who drank who's beer"—when it didn't suffice for someone to say "the ghost drank it!" things could get a little heated!

The paranormal activity now seemed to focus mainly on Jesse. He would often wake up to hear strange voices mumbling over him and see his personal items being thrown across the room.

Then, during another house party, all of the guests were stunned when child-sized handprints mysteriously appeared on the TV screen. Everybody went home early that night!

Things soon got even stranger. As Jesse was brushing his teeth before leaving for work one day, he looked in the mirror and saw what he thought was a little girl run across his hallway. He quickly turned around to look, but in typical ghostly fashion, as soon as he turned his head the apparition was gone.

The next Friday, Jesse and a buddy of his were staying up late doing what they usually did—drinking and playing videogames—when they crashed out for the night. Jesse was slumped over on the couch while his buddy slept on a makeshift bed of blankets on the floor. Sometime in the early morning hours, Jesse was startled awake to hear his friend's bloodcurdling scream. He leapt off the couch and grabbed his distraught friend by the shoulders, asking, "What the hell happened?!?"

His friend gasped, shook his head as if recovering from a bad dream, and informed Jesse, "I was asleep when I heard a growling sound. I thought it was your dog—but when I opened my eyes I saw a swirling black mist in the hallway. It felt evil." The man then jumped to his feet and informed Jesse, "Alright, man—I'm out of here!" before marching right out the front door.

Jesse was disturbed and mystified at his friend's departure, but a month later he would understand exactly where he was coming from. He was asleep in bed when he saw a black shape hovering over him, exactly as his friend had described it. The dark mist emanated pure evil and scared him to death. Breaking his lease, Jesse left his apartment behind and never looked back.

The Ghosts of Herb Baumeister

Herb Baumeister was the terror of central Indiana. He frequented gay bars in and around Indianapolis, luring victims back to his affluent suburban neighborhood in Westfield before drowning them in his swimming pool. The sprawling estate known as Fox Hollow Farms was the place that Baumeister called home, and this once prized piece of real estate is now known as the killing grounds of one of the worst serial killers of all time.

Not only that, it is now rumored that the land is haunted not only by the victims, but by Herb Baumeister himself. Baumeister took his own life in 1996, after the first human remains were uncovered on his property and police were closing in. He apparently thought that he could escape justice by committing suicide. But according to the current residents of Fox Hollow Farms, Baumeister is now paying penance for his crimes as a spirit cursed for all eternity to walk the very grounds that he left soaked in blood.

After Baumeister's suicide his house sat abandoned for about 10 years. In 2007 the perhaps aptly named Roger Graves purchased this estate-turned-burial-ground. When Roger was first shown the property, he was amazed at how low the asking price was, but once he was informed of the home's history he immediately understood why no one wanted to buy it. Not naturally prone to superstition, Roger was undeterred. He and his wife Vicki moved in anyway.

Vicki was the first to witness a paranormal phenomenon. She was doing one of the most monotonous chores of her day— vacuuming the floor. The vacuum cleaner kept turning off and on by itself, and at one point she even saw the plug seemingly unplugging itself from the wall.

Things soon got even more chaotic when Vicki became the eyewitness to a ghostly apparition. She was standing outside when she caught sight of someone moving through the woods in the backyard. Initially she figured the person was just some random trespasser taking a shortcut through their section of trees. But as she continued to watch the intruder, her jaw dropped as she realized that the lower half of the person was practically see-through. She could see right through the entity's legs as it traveled through the trees. Her jaw then dropped even lower as the spirit walked right into a tree and simply disappeared.

Even as Vicki was experiencing these excursions into the unknown, her husband was busy pulling another unwitting participant into the fold. A guy he worked with by the name of Joe LeBlanc was looking for a new place to live, and Roger suggested that he move into the empty guesthouse on his property. The guesthouse was spacious, had wonderful amenities, and the rent Roger proposed was a bargain, so of course Joe quickly accepted.

But Joe had barely unpacked his bags before he began to experience strange and unusual activity in his new home on Fox Hollow Farms. His first encounter occurred when he woke up after midnight to a terrifying presence in his room, a presence that was hidden and invisible, yet which he felt was looking right at him. Thoroughly spooked and not knowing why, Joe went outside into the fresh air to clear his mind.

He called upon his trusted companion—his dog Fred, who was lying nearby—and the two went for a walk. They were heading down the main drive of the property when they heard the unmistakable sound of someone walking in the nearby undergrowth. They both froze, and as the noise continued Fred pinpointed the sound. Without warning, the dog let out a grunt and ran off toward a figure walking in the woods.

Joe followed quickly and found that his dog had apparently cornered the trespasser. The man was wearing a bright, almost neon-red T-shirt that shined in the moonlight. He seemed to have nowhere to run, yet Joe watched as the strange character simply turned around and walked right into a tree, dissolving into the night as if he was never there in the first place. Joe had just witnessed the same exact spirit that Vicki had encountered a few days earlier.

He told Vicki and Roger about it the very next day. Joe, knowing the history of the place, began to search the property. He wanted to rule out any other explanation before concluding that what they'd seen was paranormal in nature. He could find no sign of trespass on the property, so the ghostly apparition theory remained in play—but later that very night, Joe would come to wish very much that that wasn't the case.

He began to feel increasingly uncomfortable under the gaze of what he perceived to be "hidden eyes" watching his every single move, and just as he was finally beginning to drift off to sleep, he was jarred awake by the sound of his doorknocker pounding away. At first, he logically assumed that the person knocking on his door was Roger and guessed that there must be some kind of emergency underway. But as he shook the remaining sleep from his eyes, his recollection of the previous day returned—and so did his fear. He asked tremulously, "Who—who's there?"

There was no immediate answer, but a few minutes later the knocks resumed. Gathering his courage, Joe stood up and once again demanded to know, "What is this? Who's there?" There was still no answer, so Joe forced himself to open the door and confront the unknown. Upon flinging the door open, however, he found nothing to greet him but the cool night air. Looking up at the master house where Roger and Vicki slept, all was quiet. They were sound asleep and were definitely not the ones behind the strange late-night knocking.

Joe knew now that it was someone hidden and unseen—someone still lurking somewhere in the background—and it gave him the creeps to think about it. He went back inside, shut the door, and locked it up tight, securing its heavy-duty deadbolt. He was barely back in bed, however, before his dog began to whine and growl while staring at the door. Joe watched as whatever was on the other side once again tried to work the door. The door shook and rattled several times as if someone was fumbling with the locks. Unable to make headway against the deadbolt, the phantom intruder abruptly paused its efforts. The next thing Joe knew, it was like a bomb had gone off. The door broke apart as it was forcefully kicked open.

As his heart pounded in his chest and adrenalin surged through his veins, Joe jumped up out of his bed to confront the same man he'd seen in the woods earlier, the guy in the red T-shirt. Staring at this haunting—yet physically capable—entity standing in his doorway, he was able to pick out further details. The man was young, perhaps in his late teens or early 20s, and he was absolutely soaked. His hair was wet and his shirt was drenched. He looked like he had jumped into a pool with all of his clothes on.

Joe also noticed something else: This figure was completely terrified. Incredibly, as scared as Joe was, this entity seemed even more frightened. You might think that Joe was the one who'd earned the right to be a trifle nervous after this supposed phantom had kicked down his door. But strangely the ghost was so consumed with its own fear that it didn't even seem to notice him.

Joe received the clear impression that harming him was not this spirit's intent. He realized that this person was absolutely terrified and trying to run away from something. And then it dawned on Joe that he must be seeing the frightened ghost of one of the many young men that Baumeister had slaughtered. Perhaps this poor soul had died so traumatically and so suddenly in Baumeister's pool that he literally didn't know what had hit him. Perhaps this ghost didn't even know it was dead and was doomed to play out this mad dash from the Baumeister swimming pool each and every night.

Joe was understandably shaken by his dramatic experience in the guesthouse, but he was also curious. And after relaying his astounding story to Roger and Vicki, he began to google information on those who were murdered by Baumeister. He soon found a news article with a photo of a man who looked just like the apparition he had seen. After taking in this shocking bit of information, Joe, demonstrating an incredibly strong constitution, decided to stay on at Fox Hollow Farms. Not only that, he decided to proactively explore the property—including the dreaded swimming pool.

But it was here that even Joe's bravery would meet its match. Having found nothing of interest upon first inspection, he was lazily drifting toward the deep end when he distinctly felt pressure on his neck as if someone was trying to strangle him. For a second Joe thought he was going to end up exactly like Herb Baumeister's many victims, but fortunately for him the pressure ceased after just a few seconds. Freed from the steely grip from beyond, Joe launched himself back to shallow waters like a fish and got out of that pool as fast as he could.

Later that day, unable to get the event out of his mind, he got the idea to use a recorder to try to capture disembodied spiritual voices by way of EVP. He pressed the RECORD button and began to ask questions. "Hey—who are you? Who's there?" Upon playback he could hear a quiet voice replying, "The married one."

Chillingly, Joe realized that out of all the wayward spirits potentially haunting Fox Hollow Farms, only Herb Baumeister would be able to refer to himself as "the married one". All of the young victims he had killed were unmarried, so the "married one" could only be the murderer. Joe LeBlanc, the Graveses and many others are now convinced that Herb Baumeister and his victims are still playing out their tragic lives on repeat every single night at Fox Hollow Farms.

Getting to the Bottom of
the Ghostly Phenomenon

For centuries now, ghost hunters and plain, average, spooked-out citizens alike have been trying to get to the bottom of the ghostly phenomenon. The spiritualist movement of the 1800s sought to communicate directly with the dead through séances and Ouija Boards. The 20th century then saw the rise of more scientific attempts to measure spectral evidence of hauntings through electronic equipment. Thomas Edison even tried to invent a machine to talk to the dead, and entries in his diary confirmed his belief that particles of a person's "spiritual residue" survived after death. If he could make a machine to interact with and magnify them, Edison reasoned, he could potentially create some sort of correspondence with the dead.

Edison's theory wasn't so much superstition as scientific conjecture. He truly believed that just as the invention of the radio could capture the sound waves of a human voice and transmit them to a receiver miles away, so could the "spiritual residue" of the deceased be harnessed and utilized to communicate with the dead! As far as we know, though Edison's idea remained on the drawing board and no prototypes were ever made. But it was shortly after Edison's demise that the first alleged recordings of the dead known as EVPs were discovered.

These recordings are presented as whisperings of the dead caught on tape. But as startling as some of them are, there is no real way to prove their authenticity one way or the other. And now that nearly two decades have already passed us by in the 21st century, we are really no closer to solving this age-old enigma. In the end, perhaps the only real way to get to the bottom of this haunted history and find out the truth about ghosts—is to become one yourself!

Further Readings

Here in this chapter we would like to give you the chance to read some of the resources that helped make this book possible. If you would like to learn more about any aspect of this book, please feel free to look through all of the following as a reference point.

Real Ghost Stories: Haunting Encounters Told by Real People. Tony and Jenny Brueski
As the title implies, this book is an anthology of personal testimony from those who claim to have had encounters with ghosts. The writing is rather raw, and the narrative isn't always what you'd call polished, but the viewpoints and anecdotes provided are priceless.

A Dark Place. Ed Warren
This is the book that Ed Warren wrote on the "Haunting in Connecticut". We did cover this incident in this book, but only in summary. If you would like to read more details about what occurred, *A Dark Place* goes into much more depth. Maybe too much more—this book has been criticized over the years for embellishing the account and making it overly dramatic. But from what I can tell, if even just a fraction of what the Snedeker family claims to have happened to them in their Connecticut home is true, there is no embellishment required! It's insanely dramatic enough as is!

True Haunting. Edwin Becker
This book is another anthology containing allegedly real-life ghost encounters. Many of the stories are similar to others that have been told over the years, which either proves that there is a real pattern to these events or that many accounts are simply cribbed from others. You be the judge.

The Science of Ghosts. Joe Nickell

It's always been fascinating to me when someone takes a classically supernatural phenomenon and attempts to break it down in scientific terms. This is precisely what Joe Nickell does in this book. He dissects the ghost phenomenon and looks at it from a rational, scientific perspective. This is a great book to have.

Our Haunted Lives: True Life Ghost Encounters. Jeff Belanger

Jeff Belanger has a great eclectic mix of real-life ghost stories in this book. Some of them you may have heard already, but there are still many more that you probably have not. If you are interested in the phenomenon, this book is a must-have.

Ghosts Among Us. Leslie Rule

The daughter of famed true crime author Anne Rule proves her own literary chops in this exposé on ghostly encounters. Just about every aspect of haunting is discussed in this book.

Death: The Final Mystery. Lionel and Patricia Fanthorpe

Although it mentions a few specific encounters, this book is primarily a philosophical and theoretical work, covering different beliefs about death, ghosts, and the afterlife. It gives a great framework and backdrop for the subject of ghosts.

www.people.com

This site has a lot of great information on a lot of topics, but for the purposes of the book you just read, a lot of material on both the Connecticut Haunting and the Herb Baumeister case can be found here.

Also by Conrad Bauer

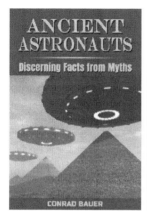

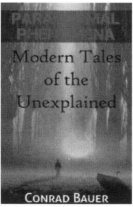

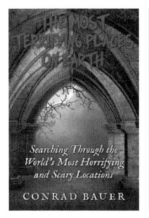

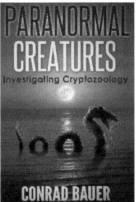